Cover Up and Save Yourself

Cover Up and Save Yourself

Cover Up and Save Yourself

(Second Edition)

Revealing Sexy is Not Sexy

Bill Vincent

Copyright © 2016 All rights reserved.

No part of this publication may be reproduced, stored in a retrieval system or transmitted in any way by any means, electronic, mechanical, photocopy, recording or otherwise, without the prior permission of the author except as provided by USA copyright law.

The opinions expressed by the author are not necessarily those of Revival Waves of Glory Books & Publishing.

Published by Revival Waves of Glory Books & Publishing
PO Box 596| Litchfield, Illinois 62056 USA
www.revivalwavesofgloryministries.com

Revival Waves of Glory Books & Publishing is committed to excellence in the publishing industry.

Book design copyright © 2016 by Revival Waves of Glory Books & Publishing. All rights reserved.

Paperback: 978-1542514262

Published in the United States of America

Cover Up and Save Yourself

Table of Contents

Introduction 6
Chapter One Who Cares What You Wear? 9
Chapter Two Flaunting Can Lead to the Spirit of Jezebel .. 17
Chapter Three Body Parts 22
Chapter Four Not Too Hot 29
Chapter Five A Pure Heart 34
Chapter Six Sexual Purity 38
Chapter Seven Desire of Lust 45
Conclusion 51
About the Author 54
Recommended Books 56

Introduction

This is what sparked this book after our family went to the Zoo. We went to the zoo today! Felt like we were in a strip club! Isn't the zoo a family place? We saw so many boobs and butts hanging out. If you have to tuck rolls of fat into a pair of pants then you need a bigger size. Now I know some of you are probably like well, we are being judgmental but here is the thing I am so sick and tired of going anywhere even to the post office, shopping, grocery store or even to the vet and seeing boobs and butts hanging out and when I say hanging out I mean literally. Now don't me wrong I am not a prude I don't believe that all of our skin needs to be covered, I am all in favor of wearing tank tops and shorts but there is a line that you can cross. When your boobs are hanging out so much and the ONLY part that is covered is the nipple well that is showing tooooooo much! Why do girls think that this is attractive let me tell you something if your husband or boyfriend tell you that this is attractive they are liars and pigs most girls that I see with their boobs and butts hanging out are ones that don't respect themselves enough to cover up and with your body parts hanging out it's pretty much inviting guys to look at you. Even 10 & 12 year olds that were with us can't believe there eye's sometimes when we are places and some girls that are size 20 are in a dress that is size 4 and that is not an exaggeration. Women have come so far as far as women's lib but women are throwing that away with the way they dress and what parts they don't cover. Women respect yourself and cover up If we don't do this makes us vulnerable.

Parents allow there children to dress this way. Do you know that not only do boys look at your children but grown men look at them also and to some it doesn't matter the age.

Think about that! Do you want grown men groping at your daughter or daughters?

Don't take this as in I am a prude because I am not I don't believe in wearing turtle necks and covering up every inch of our body.

Even my infant baby was given a skirt that didn't even fully cover her diaper. I mean really. Was it cute? Absolutely. Could I have put leggings under it of course but sometimes a skirt or shorts are even too short for that. We wonder why some schools have uniforms.

How can you have your cleavage hanging out and a cross hanging in the middle of your cleavage. What do you think Jesus would say. Are you going to show up on Judgment-Day with your boobs hanging out? I know the bible says come as you are but do you really think that it means boobs and butt and all hanging out. Think about that! Jesus died on a cross for you paid the price for your sins and you repay him by sticking a cross in your cleavage. I mean really! Disgraceful.

Teachers, we went to a parent/teacher conference and my 3rd graders teacher was showing so much cleavage. A 3rd grade teacher it is no wonder our society dresses like they do parents allow it and teachers dress like that to teach our children. It is disgraceful.

The church allows these half dressed women and girls to come into there church and worship God. Who does not approve of this kind of dress? We shouldn't be allowed to come into the House of God with our cleavage or butts hanging out. Where is the respect for the Lord. It is not my job to convict you that is the Lord's job he wants to deal with this issue, which is why this book is coming forth.

Chapter One
Who Cares What You Wear?

1 Corinthians 7:4 The wife's body does not belong to her alone but also to her husband. In the same way, the husband's body does not belong to him alone but also to his wife.

God spoke to me years ago and said that women's or even men's bodies belong to their spouse. What I learned was that even if you are not married that it is reserved for your future husband or wife. This is in every way. No one but your husband should see you boobs or even your butt and so on.

As the standards of this world slide farther and farther away from God's standards, many Christians are not vigilant enough to realize that they, too, are "slipping and sliding" in the same direction. Quite obviously, the more wicked the world gets, the more nudity it allows. God's first act for mankind after the fall was to make them coverings for their nakedness. Our culture teaches women to be forward and aggressive, to display their bodies in such a way as to get sexual attention.

1 John 2:15-17 Love not the world, neither the things *that are* in the world. If any man love the world, the love of the Father is not in him. For all that *is* in the world, the lust of the flesh, and the lust of the eyes, and the pride of life, is not of the Father, but is of the world. And the world passeth away, and the lust thereof: but he that doeth the will of God abideth for ever.

The Bible makes it very plain that we are to be counter-cultural to go against the flow. It's not easy, but it is part of our high calling in Christ.

1 Peter 1:14, 15 As obedient children, not fashioning yourselves according to the former lusts in your ignorance: But as he which hath called you is holy, so be ye holy in all manner of conversation;

Romans 12:1, 2 I beseech you therefore, brethren, by the mercies of God, that ye present your bodies a living sacrifice, holy, acceptable unto God, *which is* your reasonable service. And be not conformed to this world: but be ye transformed by the renewing of your mind, that ye may prove what *is* that good, and acceptable, and perfect, will of God.

Are we willing to believe that God's will is good, perfect, and acceptable? Are we willing to obey and make needed changes in our lives as God shows them to us? We must not make the mistake of being too proud to make changes!

James 4:6 But he giveth more grace. Wherefore he saith, God resisteth the proud, but giveth grace unto the humble.

God Cares What You Wear

1 Timothy 2:9 In like manner also, that women adorn themselves in modest apparel, with shamefacedness and sobriety; not with broided hair, or gold, or pearls, or costly array;

How Men Think

Do men have a problem with their thought life? The clothing of a redeemed woman must not give her the appearance of a reprobate woman by suggestively hugging body curves. This is a matter in which masculine makeup must be taken into account. In making mankind male and female, God saw fit to create the male with sexual instincts which are aroused by what he sees, while the woman is touch-oriented. Saved or unsaved, men are alike in this basic, instinctive aspect; the difference lies in their reaction to the stimulation of sight. The ungodly man seeks, revels in, and succumbs to it. The godly man, on the contrary, must curb and confine it. The responsibility, as Christian women, is great: they must NOT dress in such a way as to promiscuously stimulate boys and men. The danger does not lie just in uncovering; in some ways, clothing which reveals by suggestion holds greater allurement than that in which reveals in fact.

Some may say, "Well, they don't have to look."

1 Thessalonians 4:6 That no *man* go beyond and defraud his brother in *any* matter: because that the Lord *is* the avenger of all such, as we also have forewarned you and testified.

To "defraud" means to create within someone a desire that cannot be righteously satisfied. **Prostitutes** do this all the time. They dress so as to draw attention to their bodies, especially their private parts, meaning the breasts, hips, midriff, thighs (hip to knee), and butt.

Proverbs 7:10 And, behold, there met him a woman *with* the attire of an harlot, and subtil of heart.

Remember clothing which "hugs" the body curves is just as suggestive as clothing that does not cover properly. As representatives of the Lord, is it not wrong for us to create temptation for others?

Matthew 5:28 But I say unto you, That whosoever looketh on a woman to lust after her hath committed adultery with her already in his heart.

Women can be attractive in a gracious, godly, pure manner without drawing attention to their private parts. How important it is, that for others' sake women dress so that attention is drawn to their face and to their eyes, not to their bodies!

Cover Up and Save Yourself

Women's bodies are a precious gift from God, and they are attractive because they are made in His image. He made us for His pleasure, and if we are married, to please our mates as well. He never intended, however, for women or men to flaunt ourselves or exhibit our bodies in an immodest way.

Summer is particularly a time when we have the opportunity to be a testimony for Christ by the way we dress, and it is also a time when our consecration to Christ is tested. Women have a responsibility not to put themselves in situations where they will be tempting the lustful thoughts of men. There must not be rationalization that "it's hot" or "I'm swimming" to excuse immodesty. There is no excuse. If you are at the pool even a bikini can be fine for women but there are two piece bathing suits and two piece bathing strings (string bikini). I'm sure that butt cheeks and half the breasts are not supposed to be out.

What about weddings? Is it a time to throw modesty out the window? Is it a time to expose and reveal, when all the wedding guests are gazing at the bride (and her bridesmaids)? Surely not! A bride can be glowing and beautiful, without drawing attention to her figure. Saving her body for her husband alone should certainly be the desire of every Christian bride. Girls, determine that you will be able to look at your wedding pictures with happiness, knowing that you did not flaunt your body in any way but that you pleased Jesus Christ by wearing what is pleasing to Him a modest wedding gown.

If we are going to follow the commands of Scripture concerning modesty, we need to seriously consider what we will choose to wear and what we will choose not to wear. Certain trends and garments will automatically be bypassed.

God spoke to me that if girls did not buy a lot of the skimpy clothes out there, the skimpy sales would put them out of business.

Let us consider some specific questions for you to ask about each outfit in your wardrobe:

(1) Does it expose?

(2) Does it emphasize?

The following are characteristics of clothing that will in fact or in effect expose or emphasize a woman's private parts low necklines (Any neckline that exposes the beginning swell of the breasts or the beginning of cleavage between the breasts is too low.) gapping necklines (revealing when you bend over or when viewed from above and beside) midriff tops that show skin at the midsection gapping armholes (allow a view of the breasts from the side) transparent tops tight tops (Fabric that "cups under" the breasts defines them, and horizontal pulling of fabric between the breasts also draws attention to them.) knit fabric, as in T-shirt material, that not only defines the breasts but also reveals the nipples writing (or pictures) on clothing that draws peoples' eyes to the private parts white or light-colored skirts that become transparent when light shines through them above-the-knee pants or skirts low-cut shorts, pants, or skirts tight skirts, culottes, or pants that hug the pubic area or cup under the buttocks (You should be able to take a hold of at least one inch of fabric on each side at the hips' broadest point.) clinging fabric that reveals body details or the lines of undergarments anything provocative (Recently, undergarments and pajamas have become outerwear. To expose undergarments or sleeping garments is to tease, or tempt, men.) any garment that draws attention towards breasts, hips, thighs, etc., when you sit, move, stretch, or bend over.

You'll know that you are obedient to God. You'll be free from enslavement to fashion, fads, and others' opinions. You'll be guarded from the wrong kind of attention from the wrong kind of men. (Dressing modestly doesn't guarantee that the "wrong kind of men" will never give you unwanted attention, but it sure helps!) You'll attract the right kind of attention from the right kind of guys. You'll experience greater freedom in marriage as your body is reserved only for your husband. You'll be valued for spiritual and heart qualities more than physical characteristics.

Chapter Two
Flaunting Can Lead to the Spirit of Jezebel

It is not modest to flaunt one's body through sensual clothing, nor could it be called "propriety" (that which is proper), or moderation (that which is not excessive), for dressing to be sexually alluring is improper and running to excess. Paul speaks more about the need to be completely pure in the area of sexual conduct in his letter to the Ephesian church.

Ephesians 5:3 But fornication, and all uncleanness, or covetousness, let it not be once named among you, as becometh saints;

When women dress in "sexy" clothing they end up provoking men to lust, and this leads to sexual immorality. Jesus stated that if a man lusts after a woman, he has already committed adultery with her in his heart. It would be a grievous thing for a woman who is called to Godliness to be stirring up such impure thoughts in the hearts of men, especially in the hearts of her brothers in Christ, for in this way she is leading them to stumble, and Christ also spoke strongly of those who cause others to stumble.

Matthew 18:6, 7 But whoso shall offend one of these little ones which believe in me, it were better for him that a millstone were hanged about his neck, and *that* he were drowned in the depth of the sea. Woe unto the world because of offences! for it must needs be that offences come; but woe to that man by whom the offence cometh!

Let us look at this matter from a positive spiritual point of view. When people encounter us we always have an opportunity to make an impact upon them. If a woman dresses sensually she will impact men by stirring up the flesh of man, which is an evil thing. Yet a woman has an opportunity to stir up men to higher thoughts, instead of lower lusts. A woman who in her appearance is a picture of purity and holiness will stir up within others a desire to higher actions, rather than lower. It is an awesome opportunity that women have in this regard. It is like offering to all men a drink of pure, cool water, when all they have been able to obtain has been lukewarm, polluted water. By dressing with modesty and purity you are able to encourage men to more spiritual thoughts and to revive their weary hearts.

Of course, not all men will appreciate a woman choosing modest and pure apparel, for some are given over to the flesh and they want to satisfy the lust of the flesh. A Christian woman should never be pleased, however, that men are satisfying their carnal impulses by looking at her body in an impure way. Many women are satisfied with such things, and our society in general greatly reinforces this tendency through provocative advertising, through the media, and through common example, but it is because of such things that the wrath of God comes upon disobedient nations.

I've ministered in Churches where the Worship Team is full of skin revealed while they dance before the Lord and the Presence of God is not there. Performance worship with sexual persuasion going out into the crowd has much to do with the lack of God's Presence.

The challenge will be to walk in obedience to those things the Spirit of God is speaking to you, but God always provides sufficient grace to enable us to obey. Simply acknowledging those things the Spirit has spoken is a big first step, and many women never get that far, for they do not wish to embrace the cross that God has chosen for them. I am much encouraged that you are so open about what you are hearing.

There has been much written about Jezebel spirits in recent time, and the Spirit has shown me that a Jezebel spirit manifests in multiple ways, though the church often recognizes only one.

First, it is present in a domineering spirit that seeks to control men through forcefulness, badgering, and everything that is the opposite of a gentle and quiet spirit. This manifestation is readily observable, and we do see this spirit in Jezebel the wife of King Ahab, for she reprimanded her husband and was very controlling and manipulative.

There is another less recognized way in which a Jezebel spirit manifests, and this is through seduction, sensual allure and producing lust in a man, for this also leads to a woman being able to control a man to gain that which she desires. Ahab's wife also demonstrated this characteristic, for we read that she adorned herself to appear provocative.

2 Kings 9:30, 31 And when Jehu was come to Jezreel, Jezebel heard *of it;* and she painted her face, and tired her head, and looked out at a window. And as Jehu entered in at the gate, she said, *Had* Zimri peace, who slew his master?

Also, we read of this seductive and immoral association with Jezebel in the New Testament.

Revelations 2:20, 21 Notwithstanding I have a few things against thee, because thou sufferest that woman Jezebel, which calleth herself a prophetess, to teach and to seduce my servants to commit fornication, and to eat things sacrificed unto idols. And I gave her space to repent of her fornication; and she repented not.

Many would recognize the brassy and bossy woman as manifesting this spirit, fewer recognize that it also manifests in what I would call the cheerleader syndrome. A girl who might choose to prance around in front of men in tempting and seductive clothing that highlights the female body is just as much manifesting a spirit of control over men as the woman who is bossy, yet one is doing it through domination while another is doing it through seduction. Both are forms of a Jezebel spirit.

Chapter Three
Body Parts

There are many metaphors that are erotic and insulting in nature and are often used to describe women. The focus is on obscene and indecent metaphors used to describe women and their body parts. The literal meaning of the word obscene is "offensive, rude or shocking, usually because too obviously related to sex or showing sex." The word indecent is defined as "morally offensive, especially in a sexual way". Further to these meanings, a metaphor is considered "obscene" and "indecent" when someone describes women and their body parts from a sexual or erotic perspective.

The problem of using indecent metaphors is especially serious. We will look into some examples in the paragraphs below. Most of the indecent metaphors found are used to describe the body parts of women. Through analyzing the metaphors used, we can see how women are portrayed in this society. This Chapter aims at identifying the most frequently used obscene metaphors. We want to find out in what functions these metaphors are used and how their meanings are derived. We will examine the relationship between the metaphors and the portrayals of women in even magazines.

Metaphors have been described in the literary context as making a comparison by transferring a name of one thing to another. The use of simple metaphors is normal in all human communication.

At its simplest, metaphors are seen as a tool for representing one entity or event in the terms of some other related entity without explicitly stating a likeness. Metaphors have sometimes been presented as a poetic device which can add interest, wit or complexity to a text. Metaphors are, more importantly, an extra resource that language offers to construct meanings

According to this view, using metaphors is like adding spice to speech so that the expression would be more vivid. However, metaphors have something to do with our abstract thinking and can help us conceptualize our thoughts in the concrete domain.

For most people, metaphors are a device of the poetic imagination and the rhetorical flourish a matter of extraordinary rather than ordinary language. Metaphors are pervasive in everyday life, not just in language but in thought and action. Our ordinary conceptual system, in terms of which we both think and act, is fundamentally metaphorical in nature.

If obscene metaphors are used to describe women and their body parts, it means that the thoughts the writers had in mind would be just as indecent as the metaphors they choose to use. Note that obscene and indecent metaphors here refer to talking about women's body part explicitly and erotically.

This gets our minds on the description of the body of women. The reason I'm talking about this here is because so many have brought us into the most erotic thought of women. After the seeds are planted into our thought we look at women different and in turn women dress to enhance men to look at them in erotic ways.

The most important point about metaphor in literature is that it can make the reader think. All writers have an image of the reader in mind when they construct their narrative, and we can refer to this image as the implied reader. The target readership is mainly women particularly housewives and teenage girls who want to know about the secrets and private life of celebrities. The purpose of magazines is to satisfy the readers inquisitiveness, the more outrageous the reporting and the language are, the more interesting the magazine seems to be to its readers. This can partly explain why so many obscene metaphors are used as gimmicks if this group of readers is what the writers had in mind when they were choosing their metaphors. Apart from all these, there is a question that is worth thinking about. Although the magazines contains many obscene metaphors which are potentially insulting to women, many women still enjoy reading it.

The media plays such an important role in portraying women in society, once the indecent metaphors used to describe women become more and more common in everyday life, the image of women may be gradually framed as a sex object.

There is always someone on the cover with a lot of cleavage showing. The coverage in the magazines is often off-balance and much of the focus was put on the appearances of female celebrities. The reporters usually neglected what really happened in the shows or press conferences and concentrated only on taking pictures and describing the shape and size of the female body figures. As a result, the indecent metaphors often become the focus.

Here is a writing example referring to a woman's body:

Or else it will be as unnatural as a flying bomb! Or else the bust will be as unnatural as a missile!

They are referring to the appearance of the actresses possible fake breasts.

As we can see here, if the bust of a woman is large, it is often described as a weapon a missile. In that sense, the bust is destructive and can hunt a man down. We may think that indecent metaphors are used by men to describe women, but now the use of indecent metaphors has been normalized to an extent that even a woman may use this metaphor to describe their own body parts. Once this trend of using indecent metaphors becomes the norm, people will tend to overlook the underlying fact that it will subtly limit women to the role of sex objects.

Men and women refer to women's breasts to all kinds of things. Her huge breast easily becomes the focus of all the men. They all refer to jugs, melons and so many more. Is this what women want?

The degree of sexual attractiveness of a girl has been replaced by the deliciousness of food. In addition, using metaphors here can downplay the direct insult caused by criticizing the attractiveness of women as apparently they were only criticizing the "deliciousness of food". For instance, somebody may say, "that piece of pork chop is difficult to chew" instead of "the girl over there is fat and ugly". By doing so, one can avoid explicitly pointing out who is unattractive in which way and let the hearer do the interpretation. Although the underlying meaning of the metaphor itself is still mortifying, it allows the speaker to escape from bearing the possible consequences of criticizing women's appearances directly.

The examples I found were all for women, and indecent metaphors for men seldom occurred.

As we can see from the examples, the metaphors contain a lot of newly invented elements characterized by a free formation of words. All of these indecent metaphors are becoming more and more common in the language used by the media, and the use of such metaphors has a very negative impact on the society since people may follow and adopt this way of describing and viewing women and their bodies.

As metaphors are so closely linked to our conceptual thinking, not only will these obscene metaphors gradually change our way of viewing females, they will also deepen the gender unfairness.

The indecent metaphors which describe women erotically are more than simply a transferring of name from one entity to another, they also transfer the indecent thoughts to our minds when we are reading and using them. More importantly, the trend of using indecent metaphors may jeopardize the social status of women in the long run.

Chapter Four
Not Too Hot

Every girl wants to look good. Every girl wants the attention of that cute guy she's had her eye on. For many girls, looking sexy is the key to getting that attention. What a teen girl wears says a lot about who she is. But does she know that? Does she stop to think that she's advertising with every outfit she puts on? Do they know what they are really saying about themselves? Wish you could talk to them honestly and openly about the message they are sending to the opposite sex?

We must realize that real sexy girls are women who dress in a way that's attractive, but also sexually pure. That's a huge challenge not just for teens, but for adult women as well.

Keep in mind the standard that there should not be even a hint of sexual immorality in the way you dress. Does your wardrobe live up to this standard or do you have some clothing that God would consider inappropriate?

Don't be ashamed or frustrated if you find that some inappropriate clothing has made its way into your closet. Just be faithful to God's calling and make the necessary changes to portray an appropriate style. Yes, it's painful to make changes to your image, but the girls in your study group won't rise to the challenge of modesty if you aren't willing to do it yourself.

We are going to look at some powerful questions to help us look even deeper into this subject.

What does God have to say about a person who leads someone into temptation? Who should have more responsibility? The guys to control their minds even if they see sexually suggestive clothing? Or the girls to dress in appropriate clothes so the guys aren't tempted to impure thoughts? Is it fair to hold a girl accountable for what a guy is thinking when he sees her in sexy clothes? Why or why not?

Men get so clouded by women's body parts that they won't see you for the amazing girl that you are. Do you think guys treat girls differently depending on whether they dress sexy or not? If so, how are they treated? Which girls get more attention from guys: Girls dressed sexy or girls who don't dress sexy? Which girls get more respect? What kind of guy do "sexual girls" tend to attract? Why do you think girls want guys to find them sexy, even if they aren't planning to have sex? How is this like false advertising? Who gets hurt when girls dress sexy?

Is God's standard too high? Is it really possible to avoid even a "hint" of sexual immorality with current fashion trends? Can you think of any clothing styles that your church or school generally accepts, but that still have a "hint" of sexual immorality? How does this play out when it comes to a girl's decision about dressing sexy or not?

How do you think plastic surgery and liposuction affect our culture's standards of beauty? In what situations would you say plastic surgery is a good thing? In what situations is it an unhealthy thing? How do you think God views plastic surgery and liposuction? There is a woman on our block that had breast Cancer and had to have her breast removed. It's no big secret. She had plastic surgery to replace the breast and I have no problem with this type of surgery for Cancer victims. After she had the surgery it is easy to notice that she is bigger than ever. Here is the problem, she is so proud that when people are over at her house she shows men and women her newly surgical breasts.

Do you think it's important for a girl to have some Christian friends in her life? Why or why not? How do you know when a friendship has crossed the line into unhealthy territory and needs to be cut off? What makes a girl a tease? What's wrong with being a tease? This can be a form of seduction.

In what ways do you think things might "go badly" for a girl who causes guys to stumble by the way she dresses? How does sexy clothing make it more difficult to stay sexually pure? What's the difference between sex, romance, and love? Which one are you more likely to get with sexy clothes?

We all want to be "in style," don't we? But the question is: what kind of style are we trying to be in? Is it the styles of our world or the style God calls us to? Take some time today to evaluate your fashion choices, and hold them up to the standards of God's Word.

What are your motives when getting dressed in the morning? Want to impress certain guys? Trying to rebel against fashion trends with your clothing choices? Just trying to fit in with the other girls at your school? What makes you happy with an outfit when you look at yourself in the mirror?

How would you describe your current fashion style? Would you say this reflects who you really are?

Do you think anything in your current fashion choices might offer a "hint" of sexual immorality? How do you think God feels about the way you dress? Does it reflect who he created you to

Cover Up and Save Yourself

be? Based on everything you've read and discussed so far, are there any fashion changes you'd like to make?

Chapter Five
A Pure Heart

We don't hear the word purity much today. We do hear the word spoken more frequently in the Christian community, but usually only as it applies to sexual purity. We have lost sight of all it means to be pure as God intended. So what does it mean? Purity is much more than moral behavior. Purity is first and foremost a matter of the heart. To be pure is to be single-minded. It is to have a single goal, a single focus, and a single purpose for ourselves and our lives. That is Biblical purity, and from it springs moral behavior the good we do with our bodies. At its core, purity is having a heart for the Lord that isn't watered down or polluted by lesser things.

The apostle James wrote, "Cleanse your hands, you sinners; and purify your hearts, you double-minded." According to James, a double-minded woman spends her passion going after what this world offers.

Matthew 22:37, 38 Jesus said unto him, Thou shalt love the Lord thy God with all thy heart, and with all thy soul, and with all thy mind. This is the first and great commandment.

Matthew 5:8 Blessed *are* the pure in heart: for they shall see God.

To see God is to know the joy of living in close relationship with Him. To see Him is also to enjoy Spirit filled, Biblically guided direction and guidance for all of life. A woman who is pure in this way realizes an ever-increasing ability to rightly apply God's Word to the little day-to-day things.

Putting Christ first is the essence of purity. That is why Jesus' words in, "Blessed are the pure in heart, for they shall see God," are the starting point for any woman who is serious about being pure. This is not only our starting point; it is also the place to end. Jesus' words form the basis for the kind of purity that will endure for a lifetime. Viewing purity from a biblical perspective takes our understanding of what it means to be pure beyond mere outward conduct to a whole new level a deeper level. And if we approach purity as Jesus describes it, we will discover that our battle to be pure in body, as well as in mind and spirit, comes much more easily.

We all struggle, often with little success, to master particular sins outward displays of impurity. Perhaps that's because we have been trying to clean up our act while failing to see the impurity in our heart. What are we to do? We can't clean our own heart. Besides, the extent of its dirt and sin is beyond our comprehension. A heart is made pure as Christ washes and cleans it. Becoming pure in heart doesn't end with prayer. It comes as we lean on the purity of Christ, on his perfect work for us. It comes as we lean on grace. It comes as we acknowledge our utter inability to become pure men and women and our need for Christ to make us clean and to purify us through and through. Putting Christ first takes care of everything else.

When we think of purity, sexual purity is usually the first thing that comes to mind. God emphasizes heart purity. Not for a minute is Jesus diminishing the importance of sexual purity and all we do with our bodies, but he emphasizes heart purity because it is the root from which all other purity springs. If we are pure in heart, we will be pure in body too. A pure heart is an undivided heart, one with a single purpose. A pure heart is one so set on God that it isn't watered down by lesser things. Does that describe your heart? It does if your driving passion in life is to know God and live in close fellowship with him.

To the pure in heart Jesus promised the blessing of sight. But he wasn't talking about a visual image; he was talking about comprehension. The more focused on God we are, the more of him we will know; and the better we know him, the more blessed we will be, because we will see that the most awesome, powerful being in the universe is also kind, loving, and relational.

The purer we are, the more we will see. But we miss out on the blessing of sight because we don't have pure hearts. Our hearts are divided. We want God, but we also want the comforts and pleasures that the world offers. The things of this life will ultimately never satisfy us because we were designed to find real fulfillment in God alone. A woman who is pure in heart is able to enjoy the good things God puts in her life, but those things don't hold her heart. God alone has that place because her view of his goodness, love, and wonder is much less cluttered up with the junk of the world.

If we are missing out on this blessedness, it doesn't have to be that way. We don't have to spend our lives running after lesser and short-lived ways of feeling satisfied with life. If this weren't true, Jesus wouldn't have given the beatitude. But he did give it, and he holds it out to us today. Do we really want it? That's the question.

Chapter Six
Sexual Purity

Let's take a look at the importance of sexual purity in the life of a Christian. Satan will try anything he can to destroy us, and this is one of his favorite tools to use against every one of us. I want you to consider the importance of sexual purity for you and your family, especially with respect to relationships, television programs, movies, reading material, and recreation.

This is not off the topic of revealing too much skin trying to be sexy.

Sexual purity is an important topic, not only for our young people, but for all of us. None of us is immune to the temptations that Satan will throw at us. Those of us who are parents should study this with our children of appropriate age, seeking the Bible's answers, direction and strength.

In any case, do not let Satan get a foothold in your life. Know that the elders love each of you, and we pray that God will continue to watch over all of us and our families.

What is "sexual immorality" as is mentioned in the Bible? It is a number of things, to be sure. Let's start by taking a look at the word in the original Greek, and what that word meant. Here is what the Enhanced Strong's Greek Lexicon says: 4202 [porneia /por·ni·ah/] translates as "fornication" 26 times. 1 illicit sexual intercourse. adultery, fornication, homosexuality, lesbianism, intercourse with animals etc. sexual intercourse with close relatives; sexual intercourse with a divorced man or woman; the worship of idols. of the defilement of idolatry, as incurred by eating the sacrifices offered to idols.

Notice that "sexual immorality" the word is porneia, the root of the word pornography, which essentially means the depiction or written description of illicit acts for the purpose of sexual enticement. Pornography today is found on television, the internet, in printed material, in theatres, on smart phones, and even on the radio.

Some of these words may not be familiar to us, but notice that "lewdness" refers to unbridled lust, excess, and shamelessness. These are things we can all understand. When someone is flaunting their body around to arouse or attract men they can fall under all these things.

So when the Bible speaks of sexual immorality or impurity, it essentially is referring to thoughts and activities which are outside of God's purposes and teachings regarding our sexuality. With this background, let's take a look at the scriptures, to see what God's purposes and teachings are for us.

1 Corinthians 7:2-4 Nevertheless, *to avoid* fornication, let every man have his own wife, and let every woman have her own husband. Let the husband render unto the wife due benevolence: and likewise also the wife unto the husband. The wife hath not power of her own body, but the husband: and likewise also the husband hath not power of his own body, but the wife.

When you are married, to whom does your body belong? Are the husband and the wife to meet each other's sexual needs within their marriage?

God's plan was that the sexual relationship be reserved for marriage between a man and a woman. Along with all of the other ways they are to help each other, they are to meet each other's sexual needs as well.

So often the struggle comes before marriage, when young people who are sexually mature face the challenges of keeping themselves pure. But don't think that the problem of impurity evaporates at the altar. Satan will try to destroy our relationship with our spouse through a variety of temptations. Not only should we learn to exercise self control and discipline in our lives before marriage, but we must also guard our hearts and actions once we are married.

Where does sexual impurity originate? What other things can originate in our heart? Why is it important for us to be careful about our thoughts? We must keep our hearts pure before God.

How can our thoughts of another man or woman are influenced by our following them on Social Media or communicating with them by email, texting, or sending them Social Media messages? The images on Social Media are more like Chest-book rather than Face-book. I'm talking about Christian girls. This is one of many reasons why my family and I got rid of Social Media.

Mark 7:20-23 And he said, That which cometh out of the man, that defileth the man. For from within, out of the heart of men, proceed evil thoughts, adulteries, fornications, murders, Thefts, covetousness, wickedness, deceit, lasciviousness, an evil eye, blasphemy, pride, foolishness: All these evil things come from within, and defile the man.

What really makes us unclean or impure what people see on the outside, or what is on the inside? What are deceit, lewdness, and folly, and why are they listed with sexual immorality, theft, murder and adultery?

1 John 2:16 For all that *is* in the world, the lust of the flesh, and the lust of the eyes, and the pride of life, is not of the Father, but is of the world.

Do sinful cravings come from God? Where do sinful things come from?

Romans 13:13, 14 Let us walk honestly, as in the day; not in rioting and drunkenness, not in chambering and wantonness, not in strife and envying. But put ye on the Lord Jesus Christ, and make not provision for the flesh, to *fulfil* the lusts *thereof.*

From the passage, how are we to behave? How are we to be clothed? Are we to be thinking about ways to gratify our sinful nature?

Matthew 5:27, 28 Ye have heard that it was said by them of old time, Thou shalt not commit adultery: But I say unto you, That whosoever looketh on a woman to lust after her hath committed adultery with her already in his heart.

Is "just looking" wrong? What did Jesus say has already happened when someone looks lustfully at a woman? Would you expect that looking also means watching on TV, the internet, using a smart phone app, following someone on Social Media, or magazines? Would you expect that it is also wrong for women to look at men this way?

Can we fool God with regards to our sinful nature? If we sow (plant) to please our sinful nature, what will we reap? What will we reap if we sow (plant) to please the Spirit?

Will sexually immoral people inherit the kingdom of God?

Galatians 5:19-21 Now the works of the flesh are manifest, which are *these;* Adultery, fornication, uncleanness, lasciviousness, Idolatry, witchcraft, hatred, variance, emulations, wrath, strife, seditions, heresies, Envyings, murders, drunkenness, revellings, and such like: of the which I tell you before, as I have also told *you* in time past, that they which do such things **shall not inherit the kingdom of God.**

Can we really repent if we keep pictures, magazines, mail, email or internet addresses? How would we really repent of sexual impurity? Social Media is increasingly becoming a factor in divorces – some reports indicate that Social Media is a factor in one third of divorces today. Discuss why this might be the case. Describe the progression that might lead from Social Media "friend" to something quite different. How can Christian's guard them from this progression? How might a husband or wife increase their transparency with their spouse to protect their marriage? Why do you think that smart phones such as an SmartPhone or Android phone are becoming a growing problem with regards to pornography? How can Christians address this problem in their own lives? What are some subtle ways that Satan will try to tempt us into sexual impurity? What responsibility do you have in helping others to live sexually pure lives? How might your commitment to help others in this way affect your dress, speech, and entertainment? How do you think God will reward you for living a life of sexual purity?

Chapter Seven
Desire of Lust

The Devastating Desire of Lust if allowed to take its course, lust will devastate and destroy your heart and life. Lust corrodes from the inside out. So at first, the destruction goes unnoticed. Yet as it destroys, one compromise at a time, it gathers power and momentum. It causes your heart to grow numb toward God. Then it impairs your relationships with people. By the time it shows its ugly head, it often has become a life-sucking, life-dominating monster inside you. Lust is so aggressive that we must fight against it as soldiers of Christ. To not fight is to accept defeat. This battle has cosmic proportions, for it is part of a war against Satan, who is viciously fighting to divert our affections away from our glorious God and Savior.

Christians have no right to be embarrassed when it comes to talking about sex and sexuality. An unhealthy silence or embarrassment in dealing with these issues is a form of disrespect to God's creation. Whatever God made is good, and every good thing God made has an intended purpose that ultimately reveals His own glory. When conservative Christians respond to sex with embarrassment, we slander the goodness of God and hide God's glory which is intended to be revealed in the right use of creation's gifts.

Many Christian men struggle intensely against lust. Some live much of their Christian lives dominated by lust. Christian men may find consistent victory in their fight against lust and thereby be conformed further into the image of Christ, to the end that God would be glorified.

It is alarming that the percentage of Christian men that look at internet pornography is quite high. This high percentage is not inevitable and ought not to be! This is why it is so important to get this kind of message out. All women need to cover themselves and in doing this they will have great respect for themselves.

A radical change has happened in America in the last several decades. Our culture has become obsessed with sex and sex appeal. We constantly come across images that beckon our lusts in shop windows in the mall, in the grocery store checkout line, in how many women dress, in TV commercials, in movies, and on the internet. For the most part, men are enslaved to lust. Marketing professionals understand this, and capitalize upon it. Many women understand this, and seek to be the object of men's lust. So we are bombarded with images designed to draw out our lust.

    Yet sexual impurity is still not promoted here as much as it was when the Bible was written. When the Old Testament was written, Israel's neighbors were so obsessed with sexual immorality that it was commonly used in the worship of their false gods. For the most part, these wicked cultures rubbed off onto the unbelieving Israelites. When the New Testament was written, Corinth and other cities that received the Epistles were more entangled in sexual immorality than our culture. The infinite power of God was sufficient to deliver believers when the Bible was written, and today as well! With the internet, men & boys have access to a huge array of images that can provide for their lusts, both images that our culture considers pornography, and other images that can be just as deadly. These images can be accessed instantaneously, mostly for free, and without anyone else knowing. This presents a huge challenge to Christian men that previous generations did not face. The church has weakened its defenses against sexual impurity. The early church functioned, thought, and lived as a body, as seen in Acts and prescribed in the epistles. But the body life of the church has been greatly weakened as the church has adopted the individualistic mindset of America and the West. By living the Christian life individualistically, we deprive ourselves of the help provided by Christ's hands, ears, and eyes.

God created man and woman as sexual beings with the capacity for sexual pleasure and with unique sex drives. Man's sex drive is greatly stimulated by sight. God's design is that man and woman would exercise their sexuality and experience sexual pleasure in one and only context the marriage relationship. Definition: To be sexually pure is to receive sexual pleasure and satisfaction only from your spouse, and to give sexual pleasure and satisfaction only to your spouse. For singles this means abstaining entirely from sexual pleasure and satisfaction as long as God keeps you single, and pursuing the greatest kind of pleasure and satisfaction that of knowing God.

Proverbs 5:15-20 Drink waters out of thine own cistern, and running waters out of thine own well. Let thy fountains be dispersed abroad, *and* rivers of waters in the streets. Let them be only thine own, and not strangers' with thee. Let thy fountain be blessed: and rejoice with the wife of thy youth. *Let her be as* the loving hind and pleasant roe; let her breasts satisfy thee at all times; and be thou ravished always with her love. And why wilt thou, my son, be ravished with a strange woman, and embrace the bosom of a stranger?

Notice the exclusivity of the wording. Notice also what is to be exclusive not simply intercourse, but the satisfaction and exhilaration (pleasure).

Is masturbation impure? Masturbation is impure for five reasons: Masturbation is impure according to the definition given above of sexual impurity, based on Proverbs 5:15-20 Masturbation is a type of sensuality, which is clearly prohibited in the Bible. Masturbation is having sex with yourself, and thus is sex outside of marriage. An essential part of sex, as God designed it, is seeking to give pleasure to your spouse. Sex is a loving act of giving (and receiving), not taking. Masturbation is an attempt to have the pleasure without the giving. It is a selfish act rather than a loving act. It is gratifying the flesh. It is a perversion of something good. Masturbation is closely linked with lust. Lust and masturbation encourage one another. Masturbation is something that masters This is why women dressing to draw a man's eyes can even move him to masturbation. Sexual impurity includes sexual intercourse outside of marriage, sensuality, masturbation, lust, and anything else along these lines.

When you get married...the greatest gift you can give your bride is your spiritual integrity, because your relationship to her is going to be built upon two things. She has to trust you. And only when she trusts you will she respect you. And only when she trusts you and respects you will she really love you. And only when she loves you will she truly honor you. And it all starts with trust. And if you appear to be something that you are not and she finds out, once trust is shattered even at that level, it is very, very difficult to get it back ever. Be trustworthy in the smallest things, the littlest things, the tiniest details.

Because…if you ever plant in the mind of your partner that you may not be trustworthy, then suspicion dominates the relationship. Suspicion destroys respect and kills love and eliminates honor. So we have every reason in spiritual leadership to live open lives.

Practical advice: Men ask your wife to explain to you the emotions she goes through when she learns that you have lusted after other women. Ask her what emotions a woman would go through if her beloved husband committed adultery. If you love her, knowing what your impurity would do to her will greatly strengthen your resistance to temptation.

The Principle: If you have a habit of sexual impurity, you must, for the time being, rid your life of any unnecessary thing that encourages or feeds your impurity. Examples: You may need to amputate one or more of the following, depending on your situation: internet access, TV, movies, being alone in your house, walking by the magazine rack in a store, staying up late at night, etc. To figure out what needs to be amputated, ask yourself questions like the following: When do I most often fall into temptation? At what time of day? In what location? Where do the tempting thoughts most often come from? From entertainment? From things I see in my daily routine?

Conclusion

I really began to analyze the situation and I came up with this: there's two types of women in this world: those that crave attention, and those that repulse it. The attention seekers make up the portion of women who actually do seek attention through their choice of clothing.

We know the woman that is not shy by any means, embraces her curves and has the, "God gave me this body, so why not show it off while I've still got it" mentality, do we not? These women generally don't mind attention, and either openly receive the stares, gawks, honks, whistles and whatnot or fronts and repulses it yet brags about it amongst her friends. These women don't only exist amongst your everyday associates, oh no. Celebrities seem to have increased this issue to the highest level possible. Personally, I feel like as long as you own a pair of breasts, you cannot tell me that you can remember to put on your $1200 dress, 20 carat diamonds and get your hair and make-up freshly done but forgot to wear a bra. Nope! You absolutely cannot tell me that, I refuse to believe it.

Today when a woman walks by the question arises "Is there any room in those jeans!"

So what do you think, do women seek attention by their choice of clothing or does it depend?

It seems that plus size women have more cleavage, or so it was thought. I have to differ with that as implants have given small women large breasts. We never hear such a fuss being made when a beer ad on TV shows a pot-bellied man, lounging in an armchair in messy briefs. He might even scratch his butt as he calls for his woman to bring him refreshments. It draws laughs when, in fact, such images perpetuates male immaturity and disdain for women.

We have so many sexy TV, movies, and ads with butts and breasts showing. There are even a series of ads with seemingly very young girls who pose in very seductive positions. But when a full-sized woman reveals skin there is a panic? The saga continues. Whenever a woman is in the spotlight, no matter how esteemed her position, the focus is on her looks or size of her thighs or her hair style. And if she's assertive and dressed conservatively she is often called a lesbian. Come on people! Let's not put the entire burden on women for their clothing choices, portraying them as kind of women that lure men into dangerous situations by exposing breasts and butts and promises of great sex. Concentrate on what's below the skin line and under the skull. Then, when a good friendship is in place you will probably have a much better time.

Cover Up and Save Yourself

What I wear on any given day is the result of a quick calculation involving many variables: Is it raining? That's where you come in. Evolution is all about sexual selection and for women, at least, choosing a mate begins with choosing how they display themselves. As you may suspect, when your dressed your sexiest, you're dressing for other women, in a way. No, it's not a fantasy it's a competition. Is this what women have fought so hard for?

This book I know will offend many as I have done so many times in the past. The thing is women are spending hours getting ready for their day while checking the appearance of breasts, butt and legs. After they leave for work or play, the attention will begin good and bad. After the long day out how many have fallen into sin in their hearts; moved to lesbian fantasy or even disgusted by the sight of all the flesh at a soccer game, school event or even Church. You may feel good about yourself but as far as the effect on this world you have pushed women back a 100 years. This has been more than just one mans opinion take it or leave it. We all have to live with our choices.

About the Author

Bill Vincent is an Apostle and Author with Revival Waves of Glory Ministries in Litchfield, IL. Bill and his wife Tabitha work closely in every day ministry duties. Bill and Tabitha lead a team providing Apostolic over sight in all aspects of ministry, including service, personal ministry and Godly character.

Bill is a believer in Jesus Christ in the fullness of power with signs and wonders. Bill has an accurate prophetic gift, a powerful revelatory preaching anointing with miracles signs and wonders following.

Bill Vincent is no stranger to understanding the power of God, having spent over twenty years as a Minister with a strong prophetic anointing, which taught him the importance of deliverance by the power of God. Bill has more than thirty prophetic books available all over the world. Prior to starting his ministry, Revival Waves of Glory he spent the last few years as a Pastor of a Church and a traveling prophetic ministry.

Bill Vincent helps the Body of Christ to get closer to God while overcoming the enemy. Bill offers a wide range of writings and teachings from deliverance, to the presence of God and Apostolic cutting edge Church structure. Drawing on the power of the Holy Spirit through years of experience in Revival, Spiritual Sensitivity and deliverance ministry, Bill now focuses mainly on pursuing the Presence of God and breaking the power of the devil off of people's lives.

His book Defeating the Demonic Realm was published in 2011 and has since helped many people to overcome the spirits and curses of satan. Since then Bill's books have flooded the market with his writings released just like he prophesies the Word of the Lord.

Bill Vincent is a unique man of God whom has discovered; powerful ways to pursue God's presence, releasing revelations of the demonic realm and prophetic anointing through everything he does. Bill is always moving forward at a rapid pace and there is sure to be much more released by him in upcoming years.

Recommended Books

By Bill Vincent

Overcoming Obstacles

Glory: Pursuing God's Presence

Defeating the Demonic Realm

Increasing Your Prophetic Gift

Increasing Your Anointing

Keys to Receiving Your Miracle

The Supernatural Realm

Waves of Revival

Increase of Revelation and Restoration

The Resurrection Power of God

Discerning Your Call of God

Apostolic Breakthrough

Glory: Increasing God's Presence

Love is Waiting – Don't Let Love Pass You By

Cover Up and Save Yourself

The Healing Power of God

Glory: Expanding God's Presence

Receiving Personal Prophecy

Signs and Wonders

Signs and Wonders Revelations

Children Stories

Rapture Revelations

The Secret Place of God's Power

Building a Prototype Church

Breakthrough of Spiritual Strongholds

Glory: Revival Presence of God

The Watchman of the Lord

Overcoming the Power of Lust

Glory: Kingdom Presence of God

Children Stories 10 Book Series

Faith Bible Adventures

Transitioning Into a Prototype Church

The Stronghold of Jezebel

Healing After Divorce

Cover Up and Save Yourself

A Closer Relationship With God

Cover Up and Save Yourself

The Watchman of the Lord 2

By Bill Vincent Spanish & French Translation

Love is Waiting – Don't Let Love Pass You By

Signs and Wonders Revelations

I Married Jezebel

Increasing Your Prophetic Gift

Receiving Personal Prophecy

By Bill Vincent, Paula Loveless, Joseph Basurto, Dawn Vitale and Jackie Money

Experience God's Love

By Bishop Gregory Leachman

God's Greatest Challenge:

Man & His Ungodly Ways

Cover Up and Save Yourself

Conforming to the Mind of Christ

By Richard Money

My Life in a Salami Factory

Journey of Faith (EPOS Edition)

By Kevin Cann

Who Is Your Source

To Order:

Web Site:

www.revivalwavesofgloryministries.com

Mail Order:

Revival Waves of Glory

Cover Up and Save Yourself

PO Box 596

Litchfield, IL 62056

Shipping $5.00

Prices do not include shipping and are subject to change. If you mail an order and pay by check, make check out to Revival Waves of Glory.

Most books are in multiple formats such as Hardcover, Soft-Cover, Ebook (such as Kindle & Nook), and Audio Books.